THIS PRAYER JOUNAL

Belongs To:

_____

Holy Rosary

My Prayer Journal

(Catholic Edition)

- ❖ Daily Reflections
- ❖ Scripture Reading
- ❖ Daily Prayers
- ❖ Intercession Through Mary
- ❖ Praying the Rosary
- ❖ Praise and Thanksgiving
- ❖ Confessions

The Rosary Cheat Sheet

1. Make the Sign of the Cross and say the "Apostles Creed."
2. Say the "Our Father."
3. Say three " Hail Marys."
4. Say the "Glory Be to the Father."
5. Announce the first Mystery and say the "Our Father."
6. Say ten "Hail Marys" while meditating on the Mystery.
7. Say the "Glory Be to the Father" and the "Fatima Prayer."
8. Announce the second Mystery and say the "Our Father. " Repeat steps 6 and 7 and continue the third, fourth and fifth Mysteries in the same manner.
9. Say the "Hail Holy Queen."
10. Say the "Prayer After the Rosary"

Weekly Prayer Log

"To be a Christian without prayer is no more possible than to be alive without breathing. " – Martin Luther

Week:_____

Day	Morning	Evening
Sunday		
Monday		
Tuesday		
Wednesday		
Thursday		
Friday		
Saturday		

Weekly Rosary Mysteries Chart

The Church sets aside Rosary Days to help in praying the Rosary. This is the chart for Ordinary Time

Day	Rosary Mystery	Complete?
Sunday	Glorious Mysteries	
Monday	Joyful Mysteries	
Tuesday	Sorrowful Mysteries	
Wednesday	Glorious Mysteries	
Thursday	Luminous Mysteries	
Friday	Sorrowful Mysteries	
Saturday	Joyful Mysteries	

Daily Prayer

"Prayer is an act of love." -Saint Teresa of Avila

Date:_____

Prayer for Other

Who is God Placing on my Heart?	Scripture References	What God Said

Daily Prayers

"Prayer is an act of love." –Saint Teresa of Avila

Date:_____

Prayer for Myself (Personal Issues and Needs)

What am I praying for?	Scripture References	What God Said

Daily Prayers

"Prayer is an act of love." –Saint Teresa of Avila

Date:_____

Social Issues, World Issues, Governments, Churches

Current political /worldwide issues	Scripture References	What God Said

Intercessions Through Mary

"Most Immaculate heart of Mary, pray for us that we may grow closer to your Son, Jesus."

Date:_____

"Mary, please pray for."

Person or Issue	Specific Prayer Request

Daily Scriptures

"Be Still and Know that I am God." – Psalm 46:10

Date: _____

Scripture Passage: _____

Reflections

- *My heart:*

- *My head:*

- *My hand:*

Answer to Prayers

"Prayer unites us." —Pop Francis

Date:_____

Prayers that God has Answered:

Confessions

"Those who hope in the Lord will review their strength. They will soar on wings like eagles ." —Isaiah 40:31

Date:_____

My Confession:

Thoughts on self-improvement:

Praise and Thanksgiving

"The best way to show gratitude to God and people is to accept everything with joy." —Mother Theresa

Date:_____

Today I am grateful for:

I will try to give thanks by:

Weekly Prayer Log

"To be a Christian without prayer is no more possible than to be alive without breathing." – Martin Luther

Week:_____

Day	Morning	Evening
Sunday		
Monday		
Tuesday		
Wednesday		
Thursday		
Friday		
Saturday		

Weekly Rosary Mysteries Chart

The Church sets aside Rosary Days to help in praying the Rosary. This is the chart for Ordinary Time

Day	Rosary Mystery	Complete?
Sunday	Glorious Mysteries	
Monday	Joyful Mysteries	
Tuesday	Sorrowful Mysteries	
Wednesday	Glorious Mysteries	
Thursday	Luminous Mysteries	
Friday	Sorrowful Mysteries	
Saturday	Joyful Mysteries	

Daily Prayer

"Prayer is an act of love." -Saint Teresa of Avila

Date:_____

Prayer for Other

Who is God Placing on my Heart?	Scripture References	What God Said

Daily Prayers

"Prayer is an act of love." -Saint Teresa of Avila

Date:_____

Prayer for Myself (Personal Issues and Needs)

What am I praying for?	Scripture References	What God Said

Daily Prayers

"Prayer is an act of love." -Saint Teresa of Avila

Date:_____

Social Issues, World Issues, Governments, Churches

Current political /worldwide issues	Scripture References	What God Said

Intercessions Through Mary

"Most Immaculate heart of Mary, pray for us that we may grow closer to your Son, Jesus."

Date:_____

"Mary, please pray for."

Person or Issue	Specific Prayer Request

Daily Scriptures

"Be Still and Know that I am God." – Psalm 46:10

Date: _____

Scripture Passage: _____

Reflections

- *My heart:*

- *My head:*

- *My hand:*

Answer to Prayers

"Prayer unites us." —Pop Francis

Date:_____

Prayers that God has Answered:

Confessions

"Those who hope in the Lord will review their strength. They will soar on wings like eagles ." —Isaiah 40:31

Date:_____

My Confession:

Thoughts on self-improvement:

Praise and Thanksgiving

"The best way to show gratitude to God and people is to accept everything with joy." —Mother Theresa

Date:_____

Today I am grateful for:

I will try to give thanks by:

Weekly Prayer Log

"To be a Christian without prayer is no more possible than to be alive without breathing." – Martin Luther

Week:_____

Day	Morning	Evening
Sunday		
Monday		
Tuesday		
Wednesday		
Thursday		
Friday		
Saturday		

Weekly Rosary Mysteries Chart

The Church sets aside Rosary Days to help in praying the Rosary. This is the chart for Ordinary Time

Day	Rosary Mystery	Complete?
Sunday	Glorious Mysteries	
Monday	Joyful Mysteries	
Tuesday	Sorrowful Mysteries	
Wednesday	Glorious Mysteries	
Thursday	Luminous Mysteries	
Friday	Sorrowful Mysteries	
Saturday	Joyful Mysteries	

Daily Prayer

"Prayer is an act of love." –Saint Teresa of Avila

Date:_____

Prayer for Other

Who is God Placing on my Heart?	Scripture References	What God Said

Daily Prayers

"Prayer is an act of love." -Saint Teresa of Avila

Date:_____

Prayer for Myself (Personal Issues and Needs)

What am I praying for?	Scripture References	What God Said

Daily Prayers

"Prayer is an act of love." –Saint Teresa of Avila

Date:_____

Social Issues, World Issues, Governments, Churches

Current political /worldwide issues	Scripture References	What God Said

Intercessions Through Mary

"Most Immaculate heart of Mary, pray for us that we may grow closer to your Son, Jesus."

Date:_____

"Mary, please pray for."

Person or Issue	Specific Prayer Request

Daily Scriptures

"Be Still and Know that I am God." —Psalm 46:10

Date: _____

Scripture Passage: _____

Reflections

- *My heart:*

- *My head:*

- *My hand:*

Answer to Prayers

"Prayer unites us." —Pop Francis

Date:_____

Prayers that God has Answered:

Confessions

"Those who hope in the Lord will review their strength. They will soar on wings like eagles ." —Isaiah 40:31

Date:_____

My Confession:

Thoughts on self-improvement:

Praise and Thanksgiving

"The best way to show gratitude to God and people is to accept everything with joy." —Mother Theresa

Date:_____

Today I am grateful for:

I will try to give thanks by:

Weekly Prayer Log

"To be a Christian without prayer is no more possible than to be alive without breathing." – Martin Luther

Week:_____

Day	Morning	Evening
Sunday		
Monday		
Tuesday		
Wednesday		
Thursday		
Friday		
Saturday		

Weekly Rosary Mysteries Chart

The Church sets aside Rosary Days to help in praying the Rosary. This is the chart for Ordinary Time

Day	Rosary Mystery	Complete?
Sunday	Glorious Mysteries	
Monday	Joyful Mysteries	
Tuesday	Sorrowful Mysteries	
Wednesday	Glorious Mysteries	
Thursday	Luminous Mysteries	
Friday	Sorrowful Mysteries	
Saturday	Joyful Mysteries	

Daily Prayer

"Prayer is an act of love." -Saint Teresa of Avila

Date:_____

Prayer for Other

Who is God Placing on my Heart?	Scripture References	What God Said

Daily Prayers

"Prayer is an act of love." -Saint Teresa of Avila

Date:_____

Prayer for Myself (Personal Issues and Needs)

What am I praying for?	Scripture References	What God Said

Daily Prayers

"Prayer is an act of love." –Saint Teresa of Avila

Date:_____

Social Issues, World Issues, Governments, Churches

Current political /worldwide issues	Scripture References	What God Said

Intercessions Through Mary

"Most Immaculate heart of Mary, pray for us that we may grow closer to your Son, Jesus."

Date:_____

"Mary, please pray for."

Person or Issue	Specific Prayer Request

Daily Scriptures

"Be Still and Know that I am God." —Psalm 46:10

Date: _____

Scripture Passage: _____

Reflections

- *My heart:*

- *My head:*

- *My hand:*

Answer to Prayers

"Prayer unites us." —Pop Francis

Date:_____

Prayers that God has Answered:

Confessions

"Those who hope in the Lord will review their strength. They will soar on wings like eagles ." —Isaiah 40:31

Date:_____

My Confession:

Thoughts on self-improvement:

Praise and Thanksgiving

"The best way to show gratitude to God and people is to accept everything with joy." —Mother Theresa

Date:_____

Today I am grateful for:

I will try to give thanks by:

Weekly Prayer Log

"To be a Christian without prayer is no more possible than to be alive without breathing." – Martin Luther

Week:_____

Day	Morning	Evening
Sunday		
Monday		
Tuesday		
Wednesday		
Thursday		
Friday		
Saturday		

Weekly Rosary Mysteries Chart

The Church sets aside Rosary Days to help in praying the Rosary. This is the chart for Ordinary Time

Day	Rosary Mystery	Complete?
Sunday	Glorious Mysteries	
Monday	Joyful Mysteries	
Tuesday	Sorrowful Mysteries	
Wednesday	Glorious Mysteries	
Thursday	Luminous Mysteries	
Friday	Sorrowful Mysteries	
Saturday	Joyful Mysteries	

Daily Prayer

"Prayer is an act of love." -Saint Teresa of Avila

Date:_____

Prayer for Other

Who is God Placing on my Heart?	Scripture References	What God Said

Daily Prayers

"Prayer is an act of love." -Saint Teresa of Avila

Date:_____

Prayer for Myself (Personal Issues and Needs)

What am I praying for?	Scripture References	What God Said

Daily Prayers

"Prayer is an act of love." -Saint Teresa of Avila

Date:_____

Social Issues, World Issues, Governments, Churches

Current political /worldwide issues	Scripture References	What God Said

Intercessions Through Mary

"Most Immaculate heart of Mary, pray for us that we may grow closer to your Son, Jesus."

Date:_____

"Mary, please pray for."

Person or Issue	Specific Prayer Request

Daily Scriptures

"Be Still and Know that I am God." –Psalm 46:10

Date: _____

Scripture Passage: _____

Reflections

- *My heart:*

- *My head:*

- *My hand:*

Answer to Prayers

"Prayer unites us." —Pop Francis

Date:_____

Prayers that God has Answered:

Confessions

"Those who hope in the Lord will review their strength. They will soar on wings like eagles ." —Isaiah 40:31

Date:_____

My Confession:

Thoughts on self-improvement:

Praise and Thanksgiving

"The best way to show gratitude to God and people is to accept everything with joy." —Mother Theresa

Date:_____

Today I am grateful for:

I will try to give thanks by:

Weekly Prayer Log

"To be a Christian without prayer is no more possible than to be alive without breathing." – Martin Luther

Week:_____

Day	Morning	Evening
Sunday		
Monday		
Tuesday		
Wednesday		
Thursday		
Friday		
Saturday		

Weekly Rosary Mysteries Chart

The Church sets aside Rosary Days to help in praying the Rosary. This is the chart for Ordinary Time

Day	Rosary Mystery	Complete?
Sunday	Glorious Mysteries	
Monday	Joyful Mysteries	
Tuesday	Sorrowful Mysteries	
Wednesday	Glorious Mysteries	
Thursday	Luminous Mysteries	
Friday	Sorrowful Mysteries	
Saturday	Joyful Mysteries	

Daily Prayer

"Prayer is an act of love." -Saint Teresa of Avila

Date:_____

Prayer for Other

Who is God Placing on my Heart?	Scripture References	What God Said

Daily Prayers

"Prayer is an act of love." –Saint Teresa of Avila

Date:_____

Prayer for Myself (Personal Issues and Needs)

What am I praying for?	Scripture References	What God Said

Daily Prayers

"Prayer is an act of love." -Saint Teresa of Avila

Date:_____

Social Issues, World Issues, Governments, Churches

Current political /worldwide issues	Scripture References	What God Said

Intercessions Through Mary

"Most Immaculate heart of Mary, pray for us that we may grow closer to your Son, Jesus."

Date:_____

"Mary, please pray for."

Person or Issue	Specific Prayer Request

Daily Scriptures

"Be Still and Know that I am God." —Psalm 46:10

Date: _____

Scripture Passage: _____

Reflections

- *My heart:*

- *My head:*

- *My hand:*

Answer to Prayers

"Prayer unites us." —Pop Francis

Date:_____

Prayers that God has Answered:

Confessions

"Those who hope in the Lord will review their strength. They will soar on wings like eagles ." —Isaiah 40:31

Date:_____

My Confession:

Thoughts on self-improvement:

Praise and Thanksgiving

"The best way to show gratitude to God and people is to accept everything with joy." —Mother Theresa

Date:_____

Today I am grateful for:

I will try to give thanks by:

Weekly Prayer Log

"To be a Christian without prayer is no more possible than to be alive without breathing." – Martin Luther

Week:_____

Day	Morning	Evening
Sunday		
Monday		
Tuesday		
Wednesday		
Thursday		
Friday		
Saturday		

Weekly Rosary Mysteries Chart

The Church sets aside Rosary Days to help in praying the Rosary. This is the chart for Ordinary Time

Day	Rosary Mystery	Complete?
Sunday	Glorious Mysteries	
Monday	Joyful Mysteries	
Tuesday	Sorrowful Mysteries	
Wednesday	Glorious Mysteries	
Thursday	Luminous Mysteries	
Friday	Sorrowful Mysteries	
Saturday	Joyful Mysteries	

Daily Prayer

"Prayer is an act of love." –Saint Teresa of Avila

Date:_____

Prayer for Other

Who is God Placing on my Heart?	Scripture References	What God Said

Daily Prayers

"Prayer is an act of love." -Saint Teresa of Avila

Date:_____

Prayer for Myself (Personal Issues and Needs)

What am I praying for?	Scripture References	What God Said

Daily Prayers

"Prayer is an act of love." –Saint Teresa of Avila

Date:_____

Social Issues, World Issues, Governments, Churches

Current political /worldwide issues	Scripture References	What God Said

Intercessions Through Mary

"Most Immaculate heart of Mary, pray for us that we may grow closer to your Son, Jesus."

Date:_____

"Mary, please pray for."

Person or Issue	Specific Prayer Request

Daily Scriptures

"Be Still and Know that I am God." —Psalm 46:10

Date: _____

Scripture Passage: _____

Reflections

- *My heart:*

- *My head:*

- *My hand:*

Answer to Prayers

"Prayer unites us." −Pop Francis

Date:_____

Prayers that God has Answered:

Confessions

"Those who hope in the Lord will review their strength. They will soar on wings like eagles ." –Isaiah 40:31

Date:_____

My Confession:

Thoughts on self-improvement:

Praise and Thanksgiving

"The best way to show gratitude to God and people is to accept everything with joy." —Mother Theresa

Date:_____

Today I am grateful for:

I will try to give thanks by:

Weekly Prayer Log

"To be a Christian without prayer is no more possible than to be alive without breathing." – Martin Luther

Week:_____

Day	Morning	Evening
Sunday		
Monday		
Tuesday		
Wednesday		
Thursday		
Friday		
Saturday		

Weekly Rosary Mysteries Chart

The Church sets aside Rosary Days to help in praying the Rosary. This is the chart for Ordinary Time

Day	Rosary Mystery	Complete?
Sunday	Glorious Mysteries	
Monday	Joyful Mysteries	
Tuesday	Sorrowful Mysteries	
Wednesday	Glorious Mysteries	
Thursday	Luminous Mysteries	
Friday	Sorrowful Mysteries	
Saturday	Joyful Mysteries	

Daily Prayer

"Prayer is an act of love." -Saint Teresa of Avila

Date:_____

Prayer for Other

Who is God Placing on my Heart?	Scripture References	What God Said

Daily Prayers

"Prayer is an act of love." –Saint Teresa of Avila

Date:_____

Prayer for Myself (Personal Issues and Needs)

What am I praying for?	Scripture References	What God Said

Daily Prayers

"Prayer is an act of love." -Saint Teresa of Avila

Date:_____

Social Issues, World Issues, Governments, Churches

Current political /worldwide issues	Scripture References	What God Said

Intercessions Through Mary

"Most Immaculate heart of Mary, pray for us that we may grow closer to your Son, Jesus."

Date:_____

"Mary, please pray for."

Person or Issue	Specific Prayer Request

Daily Scriptures

"Be Still and Know that I am God." –Psalm 46:10

Date: _____

Scripture Passage: _____

Reflections

- *My heart:*

- *My head:*

- *My hand:*

Answer to Prayers

"Prayer unites us." —Pop Francis

Date:_____

Prayers that God has Answered:

Confessions

"Those who hope in the Lord will review their strength. They will soar on wings like eagles ." —Isaiah 40:31

Date:_____

My Confession:

Thoughts on self-improvement:

Praise and Thanksgiving

"The best way to show gratitude to God and people is to accept everything with joy." —Mother Theresa

Date:_____

Today I am grateful for:

I will try to give thanks by:

Weekly Prayer Log

"To be a Christian without prayer is no more possible than to be alive without breathing." – Martin Luther

Week:_____

Day	Morning	Evening
Sunday		
Monday		
Tuesday		
Wednesday		
Thursday		
Friday		
Saturday		

Weekly Rosary Mysteries Chart

The Church sets aside Rosary Days to help in praying the Rosary. This is the chart for Ordinary Time

Day	Rosary Mystery	Complete?
Sunday	Glorious Mysteries	
Monday	Joyful Mysteries	
Tuesday	Sorrowful Mysteries	
Wednesday	Glorious Mysteries	
Thursday	Luminous Mysteries	
Friday	Sorrowful Mysteries	
Saturday	Joyful Mysteries	

Daily Prayer

"Prayer is an act of love." -Saint Teresa of Avila

Date:_____

Prayer for Other

Who is God Placing on my Heart?	Scripture References	What God Said

Daily Prayers

"Prayer is an act of love." -Saint Teresa of Avila

Date:_____

Prayer for Myself (Personal Issues and Needs)

What am I praying for?	Scripture References	What God Said

Daily Prayers

"Prayer is an act of love." -Saint Teresa of Avila

Date:_____

Social Issues, World Issues, Governments, Churches

Current political /worldwide issues	Scripture References	What God Said

Intercessions Through Mary

"Most Immaculate heart of Mary, pray for us that we may grow closer to your Son, Jesus."

Date:_____

"Mary, please pray for."

Person or Issue	Specific Prayer Request

Daily Scriptures

"Be Still and Know that I am God." —Psalm 46:10

Date: _____

Scripture Passage: _____

Reflections

- *My heart:*

- *My head:*

- *My hand:*

Answer to Prayers

"Prayer unites us." —Pop Francis

Date:_____

Prayers that God has Answered:

Confessions

"Those who hope in the Lord will review their strength. They will soar on wings like eagles ." —Isaiah 40:31

Date:_____

My Confession:

Thoughts on self-improvement:

Praise and Thanksgiving

"The best way to show gratitude to God and people is to accept everything with joy." —Mother Theresa

Date:_____

Today I am grateful for:

I will try to give thanks by:

Weekly Prayer Log

"To be a Christian without prayer is no more possible than to be alive without breathing." – Martin Luther

Week:_____

Day	Morning	Evening
Sunday		
Monday		
Tuesday		
Wednesday		
Thursday		
Friday		
Saturday		

Weekly Rosary Mysteries Chart

The Church sets aside Rosary Days to help in praying the Rosary. This is the chart for Ordinary Time

Day	Rosary Mystery	Complete?
Sunday	Glorious Mysteries	
Monday	Joyful Mysteries	
Tuesday	Sorrowful Mysteries	
Wednesday	Glorious Mysteries	
Thursday	Luminous Mysteries	
Friday	Sorrowful Mysteries	
Saturday	Joyful Mysteries	

Daily Prayer

"Prayer is an act of love." -Saint Teresa of Avila

Date:_____

Prayer for Other

Who is God Placing on my Heart?	Scripture References	What God Said

Daily Prayers

"Prayer is an act of love." –Saint Teresa of Avila

Date:_____

Prayer for Myself (Personal Issues and Needs)

What am I praying for?	Scripture References	What God Said

Daily Prayers

"Prayer is an act of love." -Saint Teresa of Avila

Date:_____

Social Issues, World Issues, Governments, Churches

Current political /worldwide issues	Scripture References	What God Said

Intercessions Through Mary

"Most Immaculate heart of Mary, pray for us that we may grow closer to your Son, Jesus."

Date:_____

"Mary, please pray for."

Person or Issue	Specific Prayer Request

Daily Scriptures

"Be Still and Know that I am God." —Psalm 46:10

Date: _____

Scripture Passage: _____

Reflections

- *My heart:*

- *My head:*

- *My hand:*

Answer to Prayers

"Prayer unites us." —Pop Francis

Date:_____

Prayers that God has Answered:

Confessions

"Those who hope in the Lord will review their strength. They will soar on wings like eagles ." —Isaiah 40:31

Date:_____

My Confession:

Thoughts on self-improvement:

Praise and Thanksgiving

"The best way to show gratitude to God and people is to accept everything with joy." —Mother Theresa

Date:_____

Today I am grateful for:

I will try to give thanks by:

Weekly Prayer Log

"To be a Christian without prayer is no more possible than to be alive without breathing." – Martin Luther

Week:_____

Day	Morning	Evening
Sunday		
Monday		
Tuesday		
Wednesday		
Thursday		
Friday		
Saturday		

Weekly Rosary Mysteries Chart

The Church sets aside Rosary Days to help in praying the Rosary. This is the chart for Ordinary Time

Day	Rosary Mystery	Complete?
Sunday	Glorious Mysteries	
Monday	Joyful Mysteries	
Tuesday	Sorrowful Mysteries	
Wednesday	Glorious Mysteries	
Thursday	Luminous Mysteries	
Friday	Sorrowful Mysteries	
Saturday	Joyful Mysteries	

Daily Prayer

"Prayer is an act of love." –Saint Teresa of Avila

Date:_____

Prayer for Other

Who is God Placing on my Heart?	Scripture References	What God Said

Daily Prayers

"Prayer is an act of love." -Saint Teresa of Avila

Date:_____

Prayer for Myself (Personal Issues and Needs)

What am I praying for?	Scripture References	What God Said

Daily Prayers

"Prayer is an act of love." –Saint Teresa of Avila

Date:_____

Social Issues, World Issues, Governments, Churches

Current political /worldwide issues	Scripture References	What God Said

Intercessions Through Mary

"Most Immaculate heart of Mary, pray for us that we may grow closer to your Son, Jesus."

Date:_____

"Mary, please pray for."

Person or Issue	Specific Prayer Request

Daily Scriptures

"Be Still and Know that I am God." —Psalm 46:10

Date: _____

Scripture Passage: _____

Reflections

- *My heart:*

- *My head:*

- *My hand:*

Answer to Prayers

"Prayer unites us." —Pop Francis

Date:_____

Prayers that God has Answered:

Confessions

"Those who hope in the Lord will review their strength. They will soar on wings like eagles ." —Isaiah 40:31

Date:_____

My Confession:

Thoughts on self-improvement:

Praise and Thanksgiving

"The best way to show gratitude to God and people is to accept everything with joy." —Mother Theresa

Date:_____

Today I am grateful for:

I will try to give thanks by:

Weekly Prayer Log

"To be a Christian without prayer is no more possible than to be alive without breathing." – Martin Luther

Week:_____

Day	Morning	Evening
Sunday		
Monday		
Tuesday		
Wednesday		
Thursday		
Friday		
Saturday		

Weekly Rosary Mysteries Chart

The Church sets aside Rosary Days to help in praying the Rosary. This is the chart for Ordinary Time

Day	Rosary Mystery	Complete?
Sunday	Glorious Mysteries	
Monday	Joyful Mysteries	
Tuesday	Sorrowful Mysteries	
Wednesday	Glorious Mysteries	
Thursday	Luminous Mysteries	
Friday	Sorrowful Mysteries	
Saturday	Joyful Mysteries	

Daily Prayer

"Prayer is an act of love." -Saint Teresa of Avila

Date:_____

Prayer for Other

Who is God Placing on my Heart?	Scripture References	What God Said

Daily Prayers

"Prayer is an act of love." -Saint Teresa of Avila

Date:_____

Prayer for Myself (Personal Issues and Needs)

What am I praying for?	Scripture References	What God Said

Daily Prayers

"Prayer is an act of love." -Saint Teresa of Avila

Date:_____

Social Issues, World Issues, Governments, Churches

Current political /worldwide issues	Scripture References	What God Said

Intercessions Through Mary

"Most Immaculate heart of Mary, pray for us that we may grow closer to your Son, Jesus."

Date:_____

"Mary, please pray for."

Person or Issue	Specific Prayer Request

Daily Scriptures

"Be Still and Know that I am God." —Psalm 46:10

Date: _____

Scripture Passage: _____

Reflections

- *My heart:*

- *My head:*

- *My hand:*

Answer to Prayers

"Prayer unites us." —Pop Francis

Date:_____

Prayers that God has Answered:

Confessions

"Those who hope in the Lord will review their strength. They will soar on wings like eagles ." —Isaiah 40:31

Date:_____

My Confession:

Thoughts on self-improvement:

Praise and Thanksgiving

"The best way to show gratitude to God and people is to accept everything with joy." —Mother Theresa

Date:_____

Today I am grateful for:

I will try to give thanks by:

Prayer Journal

Prayer Requests:

Answered Prayer

Prayer Journal

Prayer Requests:

Answered Prayer

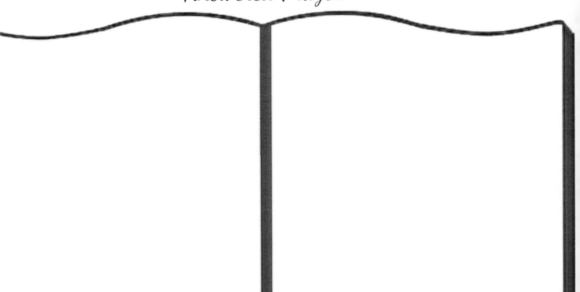

Prayer Journal

Prayer Requests:

Answered Prayer

Prayer Journal

Prayer Requests:

Answered Prayer

Prayer Journal

Prayer Requests:

Answered Prayer

Prayer Journal

Prayer Requests:

Answered Prayer

Prayer Journal

Prayer Requests:

Answered Prayer

Holy Rosary

Made in United States
North Haven, CT
30 April 2022

18754969R00074